20TH CENTURY · DESIGN
THE
60S
THE PLASTIC AGE

20TH CENTURY DESIGN – The '60s
was produced by

David West 👥 **Children's Books**
7 Princeton Court
55 Felsham Road
London SW15 1AZ

Picture research: Brooks Krikler Research
Editor: Clare Oliver

First published in Great Britain in 1999 by
Heinemann Library, Halley Court, Jordan Hill,
Oxford OX2 8EJ, a division of Reed Educational and
Professional Publishing Limited.

OXFORD MELBOURNE AUCKLAND
JOHANNESBURG BLANTYRE GABORONE
IBADAN PORTSMOUTH (NH) USA CHICAGO

Copyright © 1999 David West Children's Books

03 02 01 00 99
10 9 8 7 6 5 4 3 2 1

ISBN 0 431 03956 9 (HB)
ISBN 0 431 03957 7 (PB)

British Library Cataloguing in Publication Data

Bigham, Julia
Plastic age (1960s). - (Design in the twentieth
century)
1. Design - History - 20th century - Juvenile literature
I. Title
745.4'442

Printed and bound in Italy

PHOTO CREDITS :
Abbreviations: t-top, m-middle, b-bottom,
r-right, l-left, c-centre.

Cover tl & 9b - Caroline
Greville/Redferns. Cover tr & 9t -
Redferns. Cover ml, 8m, 10-11, 11t, 17tl
& tr, 20ml, 21br, 22-23, 23, 24, 25b,
26bl & 27b - Corbis. Cover mc, 3, 4t,
14-15, 18t, 19tr & 21ml - Vitra Design
Museum. Cover mr, 19tl & tc, 20mr & b,
21mr & bl - Courtesy of XXO Mobilier
et Design, Paris. Cover bl, 4b & 14br -
NASA. Cover bc, 5m, 6l & b, 7m, 14m
& bl, 15t & b, 16b, 18b, 19b, 21t, 22
both & 25t - Hulton Getty Collection.
Cover br, 5b, 26t & 28 all - Solution
Pictures. 5t, 8b, 12, 14t, 24-25 & 25m -
Frank Spooner Pictures. 6t & 10b - Irving
Solero, courtesy of the Museum at the
Fashion Institute of Technology, New
York. 7bl - Justin de Villeneuve ©
Vogue/Condé Nast Publications Ltd. 7br -
Peter Rand © Vogue/Condé Nast
Publications Ltd. 10m - Traeger ©
Vogue/Condé Nast Publications Ltd. 11b
- Duffy © Vogue/Condé Nast Publications
Ltd. 15m - MGM (courtesy Kobal
Collection). 17b - National Museum of
Photography Film & Television/SSPL.
27m & 29 - Corbis/Everett.

*The dates in brackets after a designer's
name give the years that he or she lived.
Where a date appears after an object (or, in
the case of a building, the town where it is
situated), it is the year of its design.
'C.' stands for circa, meaning about or
approximately.*

*An explanation of difficult words can be
found in the glossary on page 30.*

20TH CENTURY · DESIGN

THE

60s

THE PLASTIC AGE

Julia Bigham

Heinemann
LIBRARY

CONTENTS

Plastic was the material of the decade. Designers loved it – it could be moulded into any shape and came in strong colours. They used it for everything, including fashion, furniture and tableware.

The decade-long space race was won when American astronaut Neil Armstrong became the first man on the Moon ('69).

THE FAB '60s

The 1960s was a period of great upheaval. In the world of politics, the decade was overshadowed by the Cold War between the United States and the Soviet Union. There were riots across Europe and the United States as people fought for equality on issues of colour and sex.

The post-war baby boomers were now young consumers and for most, it was a time of affluence and optimism, with plenty of work to go round.

John F Kennedy made history in '60 when he became the youngest-ever US President. In '63, he was assassinated.

TV helped to promote pop bands and their music, with special 'hit parade' shows aimed at teenagers.

Designers and manufacturers increasingly aimed at this market. Colour magazines promoted a wide range of goods, suitable for a trendy young lifestyle, including cars, clothes and electrical goods.

The huge increase in television ownership meant that TV, as well as film, played an important role in popular culture and design. It brought international events into people's homes, including politics, the Vietnam War, pop music, the Olympics and the space race. Space mania led to TV serials such as *Star Trek* and films such as *2001: A Space Odyssey* and *Barbarella*, whose sets and costumes were at the cutting edge of contemporary design.

Wealthy young consumers wanted cars that were fast and fun. With a top speed of 240 km/h, the curvy E-type Jaguar was the sports car to have.

FASHION

Fashion in the 1960s was one of the most exciting areas of design. The new styles were all about fun and youth. From the miniskirt to the kaftan, clothing reflected the new freedoms that people had, especially after the introduction of the contraceptive pill.

This baby-doll mini-dress ('67) by André Courrèges came in pink chiffon with pink satin flowers.

RISING HEMLINES

The most revolutionary look of the decade was the miniskirt. British designer Mary Quant (*b*.1934) has been called 'the mother of the miniskirt,' though others, for example French designer André Courrèges (*b*.1923), brought out shockingly short skirts around the same time. The mini came to be a symbol of the liberated '60s.

MATERIAL WORLD

Most designers experimented with new materials. In France, Daniel Hechter (*b*.1938) made disposable paper dresses, while Paco Rabanne (*b*.1934) worked in plastics, metals and leather. PVC was used for dresses and trousersuits as well as boots and American designer Diana Drew devised illuminated vinyl clothing that flashed in time with the music!

This simple nylon mini-dress ('66) is shorter-than-short. Its pink paisley sleeves are made to match the tights.

Short hairstyles, such as this bob modelled by Mary Quant (right) were considered just as shocking as short skirts.

Synthetics first appeared in '39 but really came into their own in the '60s. Under brand names such as Acrilan and Orlon, acrylic was the perfect fabric for the young styles. It was drip-dry, hardly needed ironing and took dye well. Bright new dyes were developed, too, and this made possible the swirling psychedelic patterns of the late '60s.

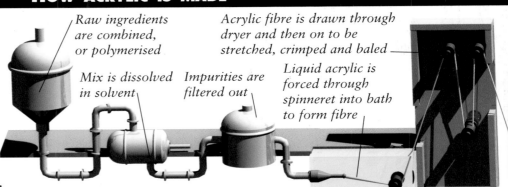

Raw ingredients are combined, or polymerised

Mix is dissolved in solvent

Impurities are filtered out

Acrylic fibre is drawn through dryer and then on to be stretched, crimped and baled

Liquid acrylic is forced through spinneret into bath to form fibre

During the '60s, 'Swinging' London was the fashion capital of the world. Boutiques sprang up in Carnaby Street (left) and the Kings Road.

Ethnic clothing, such as this woollen kaftan ('67), was popular with men and women alike.

THE WORLD SUPERMARKET

The hippies who emerged in the mid 1960s were interested in eastern religions, travel and alternative lifestyles. This led them to ethnic clothing, such as Indian fabrics, Chinese shawls and Native American fringed suede. Long hair became fashionable for both men and women. Influenced by flamboyant pop stars such as Mick Jagger, men also wore effeminate fashions – flowery, embroidered or frilled shirts, silk scarves and velvet jeans.

Teenage model Twiggy was the face of the '60s with her wide eyes and sexy pout.

7

POP AND YOUTH CULTURE

During the 1960s youth culture became more critical of the way that the older generation saw the world. Everything was reassessed, and attitudes towards issues of war, sex, colour and class changed forever.

PROTEST GRAPHICS

Protesters made their political views known through graphics: posters, underground magazines, teeshirt slogans and badges. During the Paris riots of '68, French students produced their own posters and news-sheets to counter hostile reports in the media and by the government. They used cheap linocut images, whose crude style conveyed the urgency of their cause. The same techniques were used in protests against Vietnam in the USA and Britain.

An anti-Vietnam War protest ('65).

CRISIS IN CUBA

The Cold War between the United States and the Soviet Union went out of control with the Cuban missile crisis in 1961–2. The war was averted, but many young people joined CND (the Campaign for Nuclear Disarmament). Disillusionment with those in power led young people to seek alternatives. The hippie movement, promoting love and peace, sprang up in San Francisco in the mid '60s.

Designed in '58, the CND logo adorned badges and teeshirts.

At the Woodstock Festival ('69) nearly half a million people camped out and listened to top acts including the Rolling Stones, Janis Joplin and Jimi Hendrix.

A linocut illustrated police brutality in Paris ('68).

8

Hippies combined different anti-establishment ideas. They believed in personal freedom – which included being free to experiment with drugs and to have sex outside marriage – and in political activism.

POP STAR POWER

The most successful band of the decade, the Beatles, had a huge influence on their young fans. Their manager launched them with a clean-cut mod look, with neat haircuts and matching suits. As the decade progressed, they embraced hippie culture. Their ground-breaking album *Sgt Pepper's* (1967) did away with the traditional idea of an album of songs that could be copied in live on-stage performances.

It was appropriate that the 1960s ended with the biggest rock festival the world had ever seen, at Woodstock, New York State. There, pop stars and young people lived out the hippie ideals of peace, love and drugs for one long weekend as the world watched.

The cover for the Beatles' album Sgt Pepper *('67) was designed by pop artist Peter Blake and his wife Jann Haworth.*

The early mods took a traditional suit and then exaggerated the details. Later, outrageous fabrics exaggerated the whole suit!

ART AND DESIGN

The 1960s was a period when what was happening in the art world quickly filtered into mass culture. This was largely because of the nature of the two key art trends: pop art, which took its inspiration from popular culture in the first place; and op art, which used instantly accessible optical illusions and special effects.

Wallpaper was ideal for pop art, as images were repeated over and over, as in Warhol's Cow Wallpaper ('66).

Designed by Dutch artists The Fool, *the sun coat (left) created an illusion of movement with its shimmering, moiré-effect velvet.*

EARLY POP ART

Pop art first appeared in the mid 1950s and celebrated the consumerism of popular culture, especially its packaging. British pop art pioneer Richard Hamilton (*b.*1922), for example, used images cut out from magazines for his collage *Just what is it that makes today's homes so different, so appealing?* ('56). The next generation of pop artists included David Hockney (*b.*1937) and Peter Blake (*b.*1932) in Britain and Claes Oldenburg (*b.*1929) and Andy Warhol (1928–87) in the United States. Warhol plundered everything from soup cans and cola bottles to movie stars. His works were silkscreened, not painted. This meant that everything could be endlessly copied, mimicking mass-production itself.

Andy Warhol's pop-art 'soup' paintings soon found their way from the art gallery to the cat-walk.

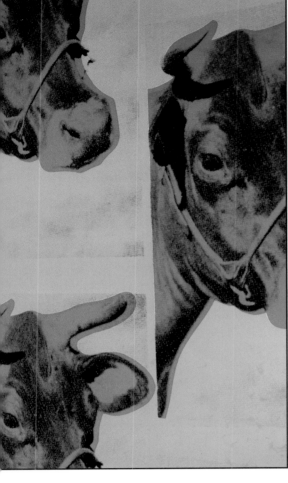

KING OF THE CARTOON

American pop artist Roy Lichtenstein (*b*.1923) painted one-off canvases inspired by mass-produced comics, such as *Whaam!* ('63). These giant cartoon strips were created from painted dots in primary colours so they looked like blown-up prints.

IN BLACK AND WHITE

Op art was short for 'optical art' and involved the clever use of geometric shapes to create optical illusions. British artist Bridget Riley (*b*.1931) led the way, initially working only in dramatic black and white. She produced dazzling effects that looked 3-D or seemed to move. Op art was widely copied, and at the Olympic Games held in Mexico ('68), it provided the inspiration for everything from the logo to the pavilions.

Op art patterns adorned fabrics (below left) and inspired Francesco Saroglia's design ('66) for the wool trademark (below). The style was perfect for an eyecatching poster (far right, by Jacques Blanchard, '66) or logo (bottom).

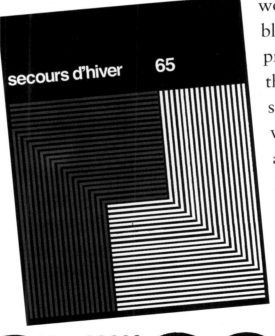

secours d'hiver   65

11

GRAPHICS

During the 1960s more and more designers specialised in just one aspect of graphics, such as creating logos, or planning advertising campaigns. At the same time, there was greater demand for graphic designers' skills, from the explosion of entertainments and from big business.

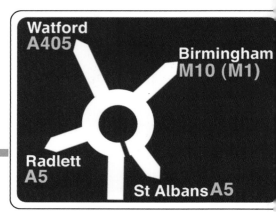

The logo for London's Design Centre award was introduced in '59.

For popular culture, signs were often in glaring neon, as seen in this one for the Flamingo Casino, Las Vegas, ('67).

British road signs were given a unified identity in '64. The colour coding and sans serif typeface followed modernist principles of purity.

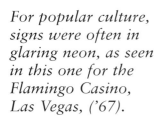

12

CLEAN AND SIMPLE

The trend for clear corporate identities, begun in the 1950s, continued. Top graphic designers producing modernist ID included London-based FHK Henrion (1914–90), who worked for airlines KLM and BEA and the American company Chermayeff & Geismar Inc (*f*.1960) who redesigned Mobil Oil and Xerox. In the case of Mobil, everything from the logo to the forecourts were given a makeover.

In the late '60s, Robert Paganucci created this update on Paul Rand's classic IBM logo of '56.

Tom Geismar's logo for Mobil ('64) used sans serif type to reduce the letters to simple shapes.

Designer Masaru Katzumie came up with a range of simple pictograms for the Tokyo Olympics ('64).

The logo for the Barbara Hulanicki's Biba boutique shows the influence of art nouveau style.

ART NOUVEAU STYLE

In contrast to modernist graphics, there was also a trend towards nostalgia and illustration. The logos designed by John McConnell (*b*.1939) for the London boutique Biba reflected the retro styling of the shop's interior, and of hippie fashions in general, with its use of swirling art nouveau lettering. The New York graphic design group the Push Pin Studio (*f*.1954) also borrowed from a wide range of sources, including Victorian letterforms and Renaissance painting, which they combined with a witty style of illustration.

THE PSYCHEDELIC EXPERIENCE

Psychedelic posters were produced to promote various underground events and concerts, as well as general hippie messages such as 'Make Love, Not War.' Key designers included Wes Wilson in San Francisco and Tadanori Yokoo in Japan. Psychedelia represented a rebellion against established society by the youth of the day. It also reflected the LSD-induced hallucinations experienced by those who chose to 'drop out.'

San-Francisco-based designer Wes Wilson and his wife sit in front of his psychedelic posters. The swirling type harks back to turn-of-the-century styles.

DEVELOPMENTS IN PRINTING

Phototypesetting, introduced in '55, became widespread by the '60s. It sped up the printing process enormously. In the past, printing used hot metal typesetting, where either a line of words (Linotype) or individual letters (Monotype) was assembled by hand. Phototypesetting allowed an operator to use a keyboard to produce light-sensitive sheets of film or photographic paper that could be printed from.

Individual letters are made of metal

Papier-mâché mould (flong)

Curved printing plate of raised metal.

Assembled metal type (slug)
HOT METAL LETTERPRESS

Typeface stored on disc

Light-sensitive plate for litho printing

Light flashes when letter is in line

Processed film

Letter exposed to photographic film

Lens focuses projected letter

Prism bends light

PHOTOTYPESETTING

SPACE AGE

In 1961 the Soviet Union sent the first man into space. The space race was on. US President Kennedy pledged to put a man on the Moon before the decade was out, and this was achieved when the *Apollo 11* spacecraft landed there in July '69.

Yuri Gagarin (1934–68) was the first man in space ('61). He orbited the Earth in Vostok 1.

After the launch of the satellite Telstar ('62), the first trans-Atlantic TV broadcast was made.

Steel appeal: the Moon landing influenced all design, from interiors to fashion, as seen at the Ideal Home Show ('70).

SPACEY REFLECTIONS

Images of rockets, probes and satellites had a great impact. They even appeared on textile and wallpaper designs, such as Eddy Squires' Lunar Rocket Wallpaper (1969).

FUTURE FASHIONS

Meanwhile, fashions copied astronaut outfits! Pierre Cardin (*b.*1922) launched his 'Space Age' white and silver clothes in '64. He stated "The clothes that I prefer are those I invent for a life that doesn't exist yet – the world of tomorrow."

In '69, Neil Armstrong (b.1930) became the first man to moonwalk.

14

Models on the streets of Paris ('69) pose for a photoshoot in futuristic garb. They wear reflective silver mini-dresses teamed with glitzy, silver moon boots.

The film 2001: A Space Odyssey *('68) influenced how people imagined life in space. This air hostess, on an inter-space station flight, wears all-white.*

The Globe Chair, designed by Finnish furniture designer Eero Aarnio ('65). Aarnio favoured rounded, space-age shapes.

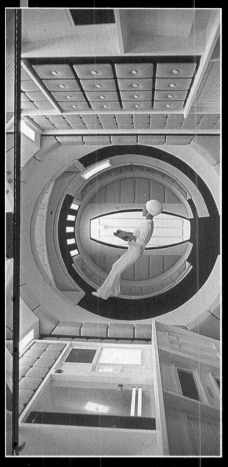

FURNITURE OF THE FUTURE

In interiors, there was also an emphasis on space-age colour schemes. Walls were often painted white. Furniture included shiny white PVC sofas or moulded fibre-glass creations, such as those made by Eero Aarnio (*b.*1932). His designs included the Asko Bubble Chair and Globe Chair, both designed in '65. Designers started to make domestic appliances, too, look like equipment from a space station.

Even television sets were given curvy styling and came in brilliant white plastic casing – a whole new look from the wooden or veneer cabinets that all televisions had in the 1950s!

On display in '61, this 'television set of the future' had white plastic space-age styling.

SMALL IS BEAUTIFUL

The miniskirt and the Mini car were just two examples of the trend for miniaturisation. Appliances and gadgets were also getting smaller than ever before during the 1960s. This was thanks to technological leaps, such as the growing use of the transistor and the invention of the silicon chip in '62.

—Vacuum inside valve's glass casing contains the heat of the wires

Transistor conducts electricity through solid (silicon)

Sony's classic transistor radio, the TR610, came in three different colours – red, black or ivory.

JAPANESE GIANTS

During World War II (1939–45), bombing had destroyed almost every factory in Japan. As a result of post-war rebuilding, Japan now had highly modernised factories.

In the '50s, companies such as Sharp and Sony made their name with keenly priced electronic goods that had sophisticated styling (usually black, with chrome detailing). Sony also bought a licence to manufacture transistors, which had been invented in the United States in '47.

MINIATURISATION

With transistors, Sony could create ever-smaller appliances. Hot on the heels of the TR610 pocket radio ('58) was the portable television TV 80 301 ('59). The latter won the Gold Award for design at the *Triennale*, a showcase of new design held every three years in Milan, Italy.

The Sony Micro TV which could work off the mains or a battery confirmed that Japan – and particularly Sony – was at the forefront of 'miniaturised' design.

VALVES, TRANSISTORS AND CHIPS

The first appliances used large valves to conduct electricity. In contrast, the transistor used silicon to conduct electricity and did not need a vacuum, so it could be much smaller. Invented in '47, the transistor became widely used by the late '50s and paved the way for the silicon chip ('62) – a tiny circuit board made of thousands of miniature transistors.

Miniature receiver ('70)

THE TOUCH-TONE PHONE

Telephone styling was revolutionised in the early 1960s when engineers at Bell, in the United States, invented the touch-tone phone. They arranged numbered push buttons on a grid and gave each column and each row on the grid its own unique dial tone. As each button was pressed, a dual (double) tone was sent to the telephone exchange: one revealed which of the grid's columns the number was on and the other, which row. From this information, the operator knew which number had been pressed. This huge advance led to flatter telephones with smaller buttons.

Introduced in '63, the 'touch-tone' replaced old-fashioned 'rotary' dialling.

17

PRODUCT DESIGNER

The taste for smaller, more compact appliances did not stop at televisions and radios. British designer Kenneth Grange (*b.*1929) combined styling with an understanding of new technologies and came up with two of the product design classics of the decade: the Kenwood Chef food mixer ('60) and the Kodak Instamatic Camera ('68). Kodak had asked Grange to come up with a camera to accommodate their convenient new film cartridges.

A mini Sony TV keeps a taxi passenger amused ('63). The tiny set was powered by a car battery.

Launched in '68, the Kodak Instamatic Camera was simple and compact. Kodak sold over 20 million Instamatics.

PLASTIC FANTASTIC

Plastic was seen as the material of progress and the future. It was cheap, disposable, and it could take limitless forms: for example, it could be hard or flexible, transparent, opaque or patterned, and so on. Plastic became popular in both mainstream and alternative culture. For this reason the 1960s can be called the Plastic Age.

The Blow Chair ('67) was designed by Carlo Scolari, Jonathan De Pas, Donato D'Urbino and Paolo Lomazzi. It was made of inflatable PVC and came with its own repair kit to mend any punctures.

This transparent TV set has a perspex casing. Produced by Sobell, it was launched in '60.

SWITCH ON TO PLASTIC

Televisions were no longer camouflaged as furniture, with elaborate wood veneers, but were given a high-tech look with moulded plastic casings. This reflected the rapid advances in television, such as more channels, better quality programming and the introduction of colour.

BLOW UP

Plastics suited furniture, too. New, high-frequency welding enabled the Italian firm Zanotta to manufacture inflatable PVC furniture, the first of which was the Blow Chair (1967). Other examples soon followed. Quasar Khan designed sofas and chairs of separate inflatable elements with metal links, which could be filled with air, coloured gas or water.

Panton's Globe Light ('70) featured a light with coloured aluminium shades, encased in a globe of clear acrylic.

Verner Panton's Stacking Chair ('60) went into production in '67. It was the first one-piece plastic chair.

The Relax Sofa ('67) was designed by Quasar Khan. Khan famously designed a completely inflatable flat ('68) – the walls, chairs and even the lamps were all blow-up PVC!

PANTON AND PLASTICS

In 1960 Danish designer Verner Panton (1926–98) had designed the first all-plastic, injection-moulded chair. Panton went on to explore many different plastics, from the clear acrylics of his lampshades, to 'groovy' interiors of upholstered polyurethane foam.

A model in a plastic raincoat unveils the new see-through plastic phone booth ('69).

MAKING PLASTICS

Plastics are made from petrochemicals that are mixed with a catalyst to form a polymer. This happens in a large reactor, where the temperature is an extremely hot 200°C. The chemicals melt together to form hot, liquid plastic. An extruder feeds the liquid plastic into a water bath where the mixture is cooled to become hard, solid plastic. This is cut into small chips. Plastic manufacturers can simply melt the chips and pour the liquid plastic into a mould.

Petro-chemicals

Heaters

Hot, liquid plastic inside reactor

Cool water controls the reactor's temperature

Water bath

Cutter

Extruder

Chips of hard plastic

INTERIORS AND FURNITURE

During the 1960s, there was no single style for interiors. The Scandinavians favoured simple designs, often in natural materials. Radical designers used plastics or enamelled metal for their wild creations. Another approach was to revive the floral designs of an earlier age. And in many houses, a whole variety of styles were mixed and matched.

This '60s living room features wicker chairs hanging from the ceiling.

POP ART FOR SITTING IN

Inspired by the pop art of Andy Warhol and Claes Oldenburg, many designers came up with extraordinary furniture. This often meant moulding furniture into pop-art inspired shapes, such as Marilyn Monroe's lips and leather or vinyl baseball mitts.

The Joe Chair ('70) by Jonathan De Pas was named after baseball champ Joe Di Maggio.

20

WICKER AND PINE

Revivalism began to appear in the mid 1960s, in the form of art nouveau and Victoriana. Secondhand furniture was matched with wallpapers that copied the arts and crafts designs of William Morris, for example. Terence Conran's shop Habitat (*f.*1964) sold a wide range of goods for the home, including furniture, kitchen equipment and bedding in an equally wide range of styles. There, wicker chairs and pine tables were on sale alongside stackable plastic chairs. Flat-packed furniture, to assemble at home, was popular, too.

French designer Olivier Mourgue created the sculptural Djinn Chair ('65) from moulded polyester. The chair appeared in the film 2001: A Space Odyssey.

Verner Panton and friends try out his new range of chairs ('64). The plastic chairs could be lowered and raised on their cords.

SPECIAL EFFECTS

There was also a trend for disorientating interiors, that is, places that made you feel weird or dizzy. This was inspired mainly by the drug culture and was particularly evident in the psychedelic murals that were painted both inside and outside buildings. Other experimental interiors were also designed with drug experiences in mind, and were made as relaxed and flexible as possible. For example, Verner Panton's avant-garde seating systems included his modular Pantowers – where each vertical foam column had various spaces for sitting and relaxing in – and chairs that hung from the ceiling at adjustable heights.

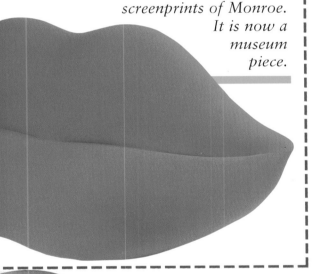

This sofa was shaped like Marilyn Monroe's lips, bringing to mind Warhol's screenprints of Monroe. It is now a museum piece.

Joe Colombo's Universale Chair ('65) was designed to be stackable, giving people more freedom in how they used their living spaces.

Verner Panton's Flower Pot Lamp ('67) featured an enamelled steel shade in a variety of bright colours.

A furniture store in Copenhagen, Denmark ('60).

21

MODULAR BUILDING

The 1960s saw big changes in the way that houses were built. Old-fashioned materials were not very popular. Architects wanted to find ways to mass-produce houses, making them cheaper and easier to build. Inspired by Le Corbusier (1887–1965), they turned to modular building.

MOVING HOUSE

The strangest result of experiments in making homes as pre-fabricated goods was the portable house. A Finnish plastics firm created the UFO-like Futuro, a completely self-contained portable house. With its built-in bed/chairs, underfloor heating and other gadgets, the Futuro could be installed into almost any landscape.

The Futuro portable home ('69).

POP TOGETHER

By making all the parts of a house in a factory, and assembling it very quickly where it was needed, the modular building idea saved a lot of money. In theory, these new houses were meant to have all the benefits of up-to-date hygiene and cooking facilities, for a fraction of the price of a traditional house. The parts could be shipped to any corner of the Earth, bringing good housing to people who could otherwise not afford it.

OVERNIGHT POD

Built for the World Fair in Montreal, Habitat '67 was the work of Moshe Safdie (*b.*1938). His plug-together apartment complex inspired Japan's capsule hotels, with cheap 'module' rooms just big enough for one person.

When mass-produced buildings were made too economically, the results could be disastrous. Ronan Point, a British block of council-built flats, collapsed after a minor gas explosion in '68.

Habitat '67 pointed the way to a new vision of home building. Modern architecture tended to be monumental and harsh. But with Habitat '67, Safdie tried to create a mass-produced habitat with a human scale and surprising variety.

Pre-fabricated buildings took off in the late '60s with instant office blocks for businesses in a hurry. The Constructa 1970 exhibition, Germany, demonstrated the best of the new techniques.

HABIT FORMING

Moshe Safdie's Habitat '67 was the world's first and greatest experiment in truly modular housing. The modules were made in a series of simple steps, including the installation of complete bathrooms and kitchens. Then the finished modules were hoisted into position by cranes, where they were anchored with special steel rods. All that remained was to plug them in to water and electricity, and they were ready to occupy. Although no modular building is ever truly finished – there's always potential to plug in extra modules – Habitat has remained the same size since '67, with just 158 apartments.

Metal frame prepared using steel rods

Reinforced concrete module is created after cement is poured over the frame in a wooden mould, or 'form'

Modular units such as bathrooms and kitchens are put in place

The final module is transported to the building site

SHINY NEW BUILDINGS

With the dawn of the 1960s, the dreary task of rebuilding the post-war world was finally over. Architects were free to explore their ideals, to design grand projects for wealthy clients and companies, and to use the new technologies and materials that were just becoming available.

This geodesic dome was built by Buckminster Fuller for the World Fair ('67) in Montreal, Canada.

GREAT BALLS OF SCIENCE

Traditional ways of building were abandoned. American architect R Buckminster Fuller (1895–1983), for example, invented the geodesic dome – a structure of geometric faces that shared the stress of gravity across its surface.

THOROUGHLY MODERN

Many architects working in the 1960s were influenced by the ideas of Le Corbusier and other modernists, who hoped that designers would create a clean, uncluttered environment for people to live in. Every building was to be designed as both a practical tool and an artwork.

GLASS MASTERED

Glass making was revolutionised at the beginning of the '60s, with the new float glass process. This meant that glass could be formed into perfect sheets while floating on molten metal. This saved time and improved the finish. Architects could rely on cheap supplies of big panes of glass. The consequences were most obvious in the creation of enormous new skyscrapers with shiny, glass skins.

Continuous ribbon of glass

Raw material mix — *Oil-fired melting furnace* — *Glass floats on molten tin* — *Glass ribbon is carefully cooled to make it strong* — *Cutting* — *To warehouse*

Kenzo Tange created this playful Olympic Stadium for the Tokyo Olympics ('64), using concrete, cables and steel.

SHOWING OFF

Some of the most extraordinary new buildings were built for countries that wanted to be seen as leaders in the modern world. American architect Minoru Yamasaki (1912–86) designed New York's World Trade Center as a statement of the United States' economic prowess. When it was completed in '70, the complex's towers were the world's tallest structures. Similarly, the sweeping curves of Tokyo's Olympic Stadium built by Kenzo Tange (*b.*1913) showed off Japan's engineering prowess to the world.

Each of the World Trade Center's twin 110-storey towers has 21,800 windows.

London's Post Office Tower ('64) made a bold, futuristic display of its gadgetry.

The Metropolitan Cathedral, Brasília.

DESIGN CITY

In '56, the Brazilian government had decided that they needed a new capital city. Oscar Niemeyer (*b.*1907) and his teacher, French-born Lucio Costa (1902–98), completed the first section of the city by April '60. The city was planned with separate zones for residents, businesses, government, and leisure. Named Brasília, the new city featured bold, inspirational architecture, such as Niemeyer's glass cathedral, which was shaped like a spiky crown of thorns with a cross 'floating' above it.

ON THE ROAD

At the beginning of the decade, the lucky few people in Europe who owned a car still had to cope with small, slow roads. But with the boom in car ownership in the 1960s came the motorway, a radical new transport concept. It was suddenly possible for car owners to travel with ease to distant relatives or for holidays in the country.

FASTER, PUSSYCAT!

Since the 1950s there had been a general increase in road traffic. In London the number of cars doubled; in Paris the new *zones bleues* reduced traffic.

New York had to build urban freeways to alleviate congestion. In Europe in the '60s motorways were built, with no traffic lights or roundabouts to hold up the flow of vehicles. The increased speed made road signs harder to read, so in '64 Jock Kinneir (1917–74) and Margaret Calvert (b.1935) redesigned British road signs.

Fast roads brought new problems for designers. Cars can't turn tight corners at high speed, so junctions had to be built with long, gently-curved slip roads.

With its streamlined styling, the Porsche 911 ('64) took the motor-racing world by storm, winning the Monte Carlo Rally in '68, '69 and '70.

Two million Minis had been made by the end of the decade. The Mini was cheap, sporty and a handy size for young urban drivers.

A PEOPLE'S CAR

Turkish-born Alec Issigonis (1906–88), a designer with Morris Motors, thought that he could make a long-lived, popular car if he avoided strong styling. By ignoring fashionable body shapes, his Mini ('59) became a huge success, in production for 30 years. The three-metre-long car relied on a series of amazing innovations to reduce its size.

Dennis Hopper, Peter Fonda and Jack Nicholson captured the wild spirit of bikers in the hit film Easy Rider *('69).*

The E-type Jaguar ('61) set the tone for a decade of car design. The emphasis was firmly on fun, with a top speed of 241 km/h.

MADE FOR ROLLIN'

Some people opted for a life on the road with just their motorbike to care for. Bikers customised their motorbikes, chopping up old bikes for parts. Their weird, unique bikes came to be known as choppers.

MOTOR PSYCHEDELIA

As the '60s drew to a close, it became less fashionable to be wealthy and successful. The hippies put spiritual development and psychic discovery above material well-being. Psychedelia emerged as a vivid and intricate form of decoration, inspired by the use of hallucinatory drugs, such as LSD. Psychedelic designs were especially popular on cars and buses, where they demonstrated that the owner cared more about creative expression than the resale value of their vehicle.

John Lennon's Rolls Royce ('67) became a £1.5m collector's item.

HIGH-SPEED TRANSPORTATION

The 1960s saw a boom in travel, for business and pleasure. New global companies needed to send their executives around the world for meetings, while families with a little cash to spare discovered that a plane ticket to the Mediterranean cost little more than a holiday nearer home. To meet this new demand, a whole new generation of public transport had to be designed and built.

Concorde ('69) brought New York within four hours' travelling time of Europe. It flew as fast as a rifle bullet.

FAST AS A SPEEDING BULLET

Japan showed the way forward in 1964 when it unveiled the super express train, or *Shinkansen.* Sweeping through Japan at speeds up to 210 km/h, the 'Bullet' train provoked a radical rethink of public transport around the world. French and British rapid trains were soon being planned, but were largely overtaken by the arrival of short-hop plane flights.

The Shinkansen, *with its distinctive 'bullet' nose, whistles past Mount Fuji at speeds up to 210 km/h.*

28

MILES ABOVE

Boeing's 707, the first passenger jet in the world, had been redefining air travel since 1958. In '64, Boeing introduced the 727, increasing capacity and forcing countries around the world to enlarge their airports and improve their capacity for handling large numbers of travellers. By the time the 747 jumbo jet arrived at the end of the decade, long-distance travel had become cheaper and quicker by air than by any other means of transport.

AHEAD OF ITS TIME?

Cheap air travel had been conquered, but designers faced another challenge: just how quickly could they make a passenger jet fly? In 1962, Britain and France joined forces to develop a passenger jet that would carry 100 people at twice the speed of sound, crossing the Atlantic in under four hours. They succeeded in '69, with the maiden flight of *Concorde*. However, the plane didn't sell well to other countries, who objected to its noise.

The Boeing 747 jumbo jet ('69) split the cost of a flight between 500 passengers, bringing air travel within the reach of almost everyone.

The jet-propelled James Bond in a Bell Rocket Belt ('65).

FLIGHTS OF FANCY

All the innovation in public transport in the '60s led some designers to wonder whether private transport could be revolutionised, too. The Bell Rocket Belt ('61) did manage to take off – but never really caught on! Still, developing concepts such as this led to the creation of cheap leisure planes and hang-gliders.

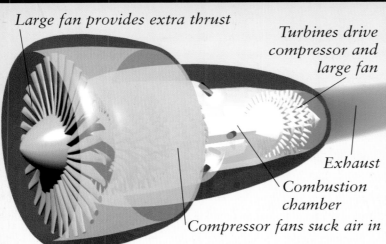

Large fan provides extra thrust

Turbines drive compressor and large fan

Exhaust

Combustion chamber

Compressor fans suck air in

READY, JET SET, GO!

Jet engines were invented during World War II to power military planes. These early jet engines were extremely noisy, wasting a lot of energy on stirring up the air behind them without helping to push the plane forwards. Pratt & Whitney's turbofan engine provided the solution in '67. An extra turbine at the back turned a big fan at the front. This forced more air through and around the motor, providing extra thrust and kept the noise down at the same time, thus allowing jets to land closer to big cities.

GLOSSARY

ART NOUVEAU A pre World War I decoration and art style based on naturalistic plant motifs and sinuous curves.

ESTABLISHMENT The part of society that holds the power and is considered to have traditional ideas and values.

FLAT-PACK FURNITURE Furniture designed for self-assembly. It is easier for shops to store and cheaper for consumers to buy.

GEODESIC DOME A light, strong dome, consisting of a grid of (usually) triangular facets.

INJECTION MOULDING Technique for mass-producing thermoplastic products.

KAFTAN Loosely-cut, ankle-length garment based on African and Arabic tribal wear.

LINOCUT A print made by cutting the design in relief on linoleum (a tough floor tile).

MASS-PRODUCTION The production of standardized goods in large quantities, usually by machine.

MODERNISM An international movement in architecture and design that promoted utility and rejected fussy decoration.

OP ART Art style that creates an optical illusion.

POP ART Art that draws inspiration from consumerism and popular culture.

PRE-FABRICATED Describes buildings created from readymade modular units that are slotted together on site.

PSYCHEDELIA Visual or sound effects inspired by a mind-bending drug, such as LSD.

PVC Short for polyvinyl chloride. A tough, shiny and weather-resistant plastic.

REINFORCED CONCRETE Concrete strengthened by having steel bars or wires embedded in it.

REVIVALISM Revisiting styles and fashions of the past.

SANS SERIF A typeface that does not have decorative serifs on the top and bottom of the letters.

SILKSCREENING Process of printing where ink is applied to stretched fabric. Stencils keep some areas ink-free.

TRANSISTOR A piece of silicon used to conduct electricity.

30

DESIGN HIGHLIGHTS

- *Grange: Kenwood Chef food mixer*
- *Panton: Stacking Chair*

1

- *E-type Jaguar*
- *Bell Rocket Belt*
- *First Archigram broadsheet*

1

- *Ulm school rework Lufthansa's identity*
- *Pier Giacomo & Achille Castiglioni: Arco lamp*

1

- *Gropius: Pan-Am Building* •*Quant starts Ginger Group*
- *Murdoch: Spotty Chair*

1

- *Cardin: Space Age*
- *Geismar: Mobil logo*
- *Conran opens Habitat*
- *Olympic Stadium, Tokyo* •*Biba opens*

1

- *Yves Saint Laurent: Mondrian dress*
- *Aarnio: Globe Chair*
- *Mourgue: Djinn Chair*

1

- *Warhol: Cow Wallpaper*
- *Saroglia: wool mark*
- *Seifert: Centre Point, London* •*Magistretti: Chimera Light*

1

- *Safdie: Habitat '67*
- *Blow Chair*
- *Panton: Flower Pot Lamp*

1

- *Grange: Kodak Instamatic Camera*
- *Archigram: the Instant City*
- *McConnell: Biba logo*

1

- *Futuro portable home*
- *Archizoom: Mies Chair*
- *Colombo: Tube-chair*
- *Pesce: Up chair series*

1

TIMELINE

	WORLD EVENTS	TECHNOLOGY	FAMOUS PEOPLE	ART & MEDIA
0	•Belgian Congo granted independence	•Laser invented •US submarine Triton circumnavigates the world underwater	•Leonid Brezhnev President of USSR •Madonna born	•Yves Klein: Anthropométries •Alfred Hitchcock: Pyscho
1	•Bay of Pigs invasion of Cuba •Berlin Wall built	•Yuri Gagarin is the first man in space •Renault 4 first produced	•Ernest Hemingway commits suicide •Ballet star Nureyev defects from USSR	•Claes Oldenburg opens 'The Store', selling plastic replicas of food
2	•Cuban missile crisis •Algeria independent from France	•Telstar satellite launched •Silicon breast implant	•Death of Marilyn Monroe •Georges Pompidou is French PM	•Warhol: One Hundred Campbell's Soup Cans •Burgess: A Clockwork Orange
3	•Nuclear Test Ban Treaty, signed by USSR, UK & USA	•Philips introduce audio cassette tapes •Valium introduced in USA	•Assassination of John F Kennedy •Bruce Reynolds leads the Great Train Robbery	•Roy Lichtenstein: Whaam! •Beach Boys: Surfin' USA
4	•UN sanctions against South Africa •Vietnam War begins •PLO formed •Olympics, Tokyo	•Word processor invented •Moog synthesizer invented	•Muhammad Ali world heavyweight champion •Nelson Mandela jailed in South Africa	•The Hollies: In the Hollies Style •Goldfinger •A Fistful of Dollars
5	•India and Pakistan at war over Kashmir •End of capital punishment in UK	•Completion of France–Italy road tunnel through Mt Blanc	•Assassination of Malcolm X	•Bridget Riley: Arrest I •Doctor Zhivago •The Sound of Music
6	•Cultural revolution in China	•Fuel-injection introduced for car engines in UK	•England football team win World Cup	•David Hemmings: Blow-Up •Bob Dylan: Blonde on Blonde
7	•Six-Day War between Arabs and Israelis	•First heart transplant •Dolby introduces noise reduction system for stereos	•Che Guevara killed in Bolivia •Artists Gilbert & George first meet	•Disney: Jungle Book •Beatles: Sgt Pepper's Lonely Hearts Club Band •The Doors: The Doors
8	•USSR invades Czechoslovakia •Students riot in Paris •Tet offensive, Vietnam •Olympics, Mexico	•Aswan Dam completed •Collapse at Ronan Point	•Assassination of Martin Luther King Jr •Yuri Gagarin dies in plane crash	•Chitty Chitty Bang Bang •2001: A Space Odyssey •Marvin Gaye: I Heard it through the Grapevine
9	•Stonewall Uprising: beginning of Gay Rights movement	•Neil Armstrong takes first moon walk •Concorde's maiden flight	•Marriage of John Lennon & Yoko Ono •Ronald & Reggie Kray jailed	•Woodstock music festival, USA

INDEX

32